M000074007

THE
TOTALLY NUTS
COOKBOOK

THE
TOTALLY
NUTS
COOKBOOK

by Helene Siegel

Illustrated by Caroline Vibbert

CELESTIAL ARTS
BERKELEY, CALIFORNIA

The Totally Nuts Cookbook is produced by becker&mayer!, Ltd.

Printed in Singapore.

Cover design and illustration: Bob Greisen
Interior design and typesetting: Susan Hernday
Interior illustrations: Carolyn Vibbert

Library of Congress Cataloging-in-Publication Data
Siegel, Helene.
The Totally Nuts Cookbook / by Helene Siegel; illustrated by
Caroline Vibbert.
    p.   cm.
  ISBN 0-89087-835-8
    1. Cookery (Nuts)   I. Title.
TX814.S54   1997   97-24699
641.6'45--dc21   CIP

Celestial Arts Publishing
P.O. Box 7123
Berkeley, CA 94707

Look for all 24 *Totally* cookbooks in your local store!

SOMETIMES YOU FEEL LIKE A NUT...

CONTENTS

INTRODUCTION

Nuts are as ancient as civilization itself—evidence of almonds and pistachios dating back 10,000 years has been found in a village in eastern Turkey, and references to both can be found in the Bible.

The appeal of nuts for the earliest people is not difficult to imagine. Nuts are easy to gather and store. Their shells offer natural protection and they can be stored without preservatives against future famine or other catastrophe.

Why, in late 20th-century America, with a dozen varieties of frozen waffles in the supermarket, bagels at the corner store, and pizza just a phone call away, do nuts still appeal? Nuts toasted and tossed into a salad or baked into a cookie add that extra dollop of flavor and richness our appetites crave. Not to mention the crunch factor!

Here in California, a wide variety of high-quality nuts is available, shelled and ready for cooking year round. I like to stock my freezer with pecans, walnuts, pine nuts, a few types of almonds, shredded coconut, and a small bag of macadamias for impromptu baking. For a quick after-school snack, I sometimes place a selection of nuts, coconut, and dried fruits (raisins, cranberries, cherries, apricots) on a cutting board for the kids to create their own trail mix. Voilà, a healthy treat!

Nuts are always wonderful, but in baking they are irreplaceable. No doubt about it, the world would be a thinner place without our pecan pies, chocolate-covered almonds, walnut-stuffed brownies, and delicate almond pastries and tarts. So begin with dessert, and work your way backward. Sounds nutty, but what the hell, go for it!

What Is a Nut?
True nuts grow on trees. A nut is a fruit surrounded by a dry, hard shell that must be cracked open to release the lone kernel, or "nut." Though commonly considered as such, coconuts, pine nuts, and peanuts are not true nuts.

SALADS
AND
NIBBLES

LENTIL WALNUT SALAD

The earthiness of lentils, radishes, and nuts combines beautifully in this soul-satisfying winter salad.

1 cup small green lentils
water to cover
½ large red onion, chopped
½ cup trimmed, diced radishes
1 cup walnuts, toasted and chopped
¼ cup red wine vinegar
½ teaspoon Dijon mustard
½ cup olive oil
salt and freshly ground pepper
½ cup crumbled feta cheese

Rinse the lentils, and place in a medium saucepan. Generously cover with water. Bring to a boil, reduce to a simmer, and cook, uncovered, about 25 minutes, until done.

Meanwhile, place the onion, radishes, and walnuts in a large bowl. In a small bowl, whisk together the red wine vinegar, mustard, oil, salt, and pepper, and reserve.

Strain the warm lentils, and transfer to bowl with nuts. Toss, pour on dressing, and toss again to coat evenly. Sprinkle with feta, mix, and serve or chill. Lentil salad will keep about 2 days in the refrigerator. Bring back to room temperature before serving.

SERVES 6 TO 8

Toasting Nuts

Almost all nuts benefit from a quick toasting to bring their oils to the surface and develop flavor. Spread nuts on a baking sheet, and toast in a 350-degree F oven, shaking the pan occasionally, until nuts are golden and fragrant, 7 to 15 minutes. Nuts can also be toasted in a dry pan over medium-low heat on the stovetop. Stay nearby, and keep shaking the pan to toast evenly and prevent scorching.

ROASTED PEAR HAZELNUT SALAD

A delicate fruit and nut salad like this is a nice beginning for a romantic dinner for two.

2 teaspoons butter
1 pear, peeled, cored, and halved
     lengthwise
1 large Belgian endive, washed and sliced
1 head frisée lettuce, washed and torn
¼ cup lemon juice
2 tablespoons white wine vinegar
1 teaspoon honey
¼ cup vegetable oil
salt
½ cup hazelnuts, toasted, peeled, and
     roughly chopped

Preheat oven to 400 degrees F.

Place butter in a small ceramic roasting pan, and place in the oven to melt. Swirl to coat pan, and add pear halves. Turn pears to coat evenly, and bake, uncovered, 30 to 40 minutes, until soft. Keep warm.

Combine the endive and frisée in bowl. In another small bowl, whisk together lemon juice, vinegar, honey, oil, and salt. Pour all but about 3 tablespoons dressing over salad, and toss to coat. Arrange salad on two serving plates.

Thinly slice warm pears lengthwise, leaving stem end attached. Fan slices and place over each salad. Sprinkle each with nuts. Spoon remaining dressing over pears and nuts. Serve immediately.

SERVES 2

Storing Nuts
Store all shelled nuts in an airtight container in the freezer. If fresh when purchased, nuts can keep as long as a year. They can be used directly from the freezer for baking, without defrosting.

GREEN BEANS AND HAZELNUT SALAD

An elegant salad like this one is a good opportunity to use that high quality nut oil you may be saving in the pantry.

12 ounces French green beans, trimmed
salt
3 tablespoons heavy cream
1 tablespoon hazelnut, walnut,
   or peanut oil
1 teaspoon Dijon mustard
juice of ½ lemon
freshly ground pepper
⅓ cup hazelnuts

Blanch the beans in boiling salted water about 4 minutes, or microwave with about 1 tablespoon water in a covered dish 2 minutes at full power. Drain, rinse with cold water, and pat dry. Transfer beans to bowl or serving dish, and chill.

In a small bowl, whisk together cream, nut oil, mustard, lemon, salt, and pepper. Pour over the beans. Toss to coat evenly.

With a sharp paring knife, thinly slice hazelnuts. Toast in small, dry skillet over medium-high heat, shaking frequently, until golden but not brown. Set aside to cool. When cool, remove any loose or burnt skins. Scatter nuts over beans, and serve or chill until serving time.

SERVES 3 TO 4

Chopping and Grinding Nuts
Unless the quantity is great, roughly chop nuts by hand with a large chef's knife to better control the size. For grinding nuts, the food processor is excellent. Stay nearby and pulse until you get the feeling for how long it takes, because overprocessing can result in nut butter if too much oil is released. Ground nuts may also be frozen.

GREEN APPLES AND WALNUT SALAD

This pretty salad is a mélange of tastes and textures, from crunchy nuts and tart green apples to rich, salty blue cheese. A sure hit for blue cheese fans—substitute Stilton, Gorgonzola, or Roquefort as you wish.

1 tablespoon butter
1 cup walnut pieces
1 tablespoon sugar
2 Granny Smith apples, peeled, cored, and julienned
2 large Belgian endives, thinly sliced
½ cup crumbled blue cheese
2 tablespoons sherry wine vinegar
2 tablespoons olive oil
salt and freshly ground pepper

Melt the butter in a small skillet over moderate heat. Add walnuts and sugar, and cook, stirring occasionally, until crisp, about 2 minutes. Drain on paper towels.

In a large bowl, combine apples, endives, blue cheese, and walnuts. In a small bowl, whisk together sherry vinegar, olive oil, salt, and pepper. Pour over salad, toss to coat evenly, and serve.

SERVES 4

WARM GOAT CHEESE
ALMOND SALAD

*Savory warm goat cheese on top of crisp
greens is a typical French dinner starter. With
some crusty bread, it also makes a nice, light
lunch.*

1 (5½-ounce) log soft goat cheese
⅓ cup coarsely ground roasted almonds
4 cups mixed, cleaned salad greens
½ cup cherry tomatoes, halved
1 tablespoon lemon juice
2 tablespoons red wine vinegar
½ cup olive oil
salt and freshly ground pepper
olive oil for drizzling

Carefully cut the goat cheese across width into 4 slices. Place almonds in small bowl, and dip each slice to coat evenly. Chill 1 hour.

Preheat broiler and arrange rack 6 inches from heat.

Place salad greens and tomatoes in bowl. In another bowl, whisk together lemon juice, vinegar, olive oil, salt, and pepper. Pour over salad, and toss to coat evenly. Divide and arrange salad on four serving plates.

Place goat cheese on baking sheet and lightly drizzle with olive oil. Broil less than 1 minute per side, to soften cheese (being careful not to burn nuts). With a spatula, carefully transfer each to a salad and serve while warm.

SERVES 4

SPICED ALMONDS

Homemade spiced nuts are much fresher (and less salty) than those sold in stores. Adjust the seasonings to taste, and feel free to substitute the nut of your choice.

½ teaspoon salt
½ teaspoon cayenne
½ teaspoon paprika
¼ teaspoon ground cumin
3 tablespoons olive oil
2 cups blanched whole almonds

In a small bowl, combine salt, cayenne, paprika, and cumin.

Heat the oil in medium skillet over low heat. Add almonds and spice mix, and cook, stirring frequently, until golden, about 5 minutes. Transfer to paper towels to drain, and pat dry. Taste, add salt to taste, and transfer to serving dish.

MAKES 2 CUPS, ENOUGH FOR 8

NUTTY SIDES
AND
SPREADS

RICE PILAF WITH SPINACH AND PINE NUTS

A deeply flavored, substantial side dish such as this is satisfying enough to make into a small vegetarian meal, with a salad or one more side dish.

4 tablespoons olive oil
¼ cup pine nuts
1 (10-ounce) bag washed spinach
coarse salt
½ medium onion, chopped
2 garlic cloves, minced
1 cup long-grained rice
2 cups hot chicken stock
freshly ground pepper

Heat 1 tablespoon of the oil in a large skillet over medium heat. Sauté the pine nuts until golden, 2 minutes. Remove with slotted spoon. Heat an additional tablespoon of oil in the pan. Turn heat to high, and cook spinach with salt in batches, turning frequently, until all the spinach is wilted. Let cool. When cool enough to handle, chop spinach.

Heat the remaining oil in a medium saucepan over medium heat. Sauté onion, garlic, and rice, stirring frequently, until rice is golden, about 5 minutes. Pour in hot stock. Cover, reduce to simmer, and cook 25 minutes, until liquid is absorbed. Stir in chopped spinach, pine nuts, salt, and pepper. Cover, remove from heat, and let sit 5 minutes to heat through. Fluff and serve.

SERVES 4

Pine Nuts
Pine nuts, also known as pignolias *in Europe and* piñons *in the American Southwest, are the seeds of a Mediterranean stone pine tree. The tiny white nut is used in the cuisines of Italy, Spain, Greece, and Turkey and other Middle Eastern countries.*
Because of their high price, pine nuts are a bit of a delicacy here. They have one of the highest fat contents of any nut. Pine nuts are available in the supermarket and in Italian and Greek markets.

HAROSET

Chopped apples and walnuts are a symbolic food at the traditional Jewish Passover meal or seder. They represent the mortar used to build the pyramids. Haroset is delicious spread on matzo or crackers.

2 Fuji, gala, *or* Granny Smith apples, peeled, cored, and diced
¾ cup walnuts, coarsely chopped
¼ cup raisins, chopped
½ teaspoon ground cinnamon
1½ tablespoons honey
juice of 1 lemon
1 tablespoon sweet red wine

Place all of the ingredients in a bowl. Mix to combine, and reserve in the refrigerator as long as 1 day.

MAKES 2 CUPS, ENOUGH FOR 4 TO 6

THAI PEANUT SLAW

Here is a refreshing, easy, low-fat accompaniment to summer barbecues.

1 green cabbage, cored and thinly sliced
4 scallions, cut in 1-inch lengths and
    slivered
½ cup chopped fresh cilantro
1 serrano chile, seeded and diced
1 cup dry roasted unsalted peanuts
juice of 2 oranges
juice of 2 limes
1½ tablespoons brown sugar
¼ cup Thai fish sauce

In a large bowl, combine cabbage, scallions, cilantro, serrano, and peanuts. Mix well.

In a small bowl, whisk together orange and lime juices, brown sugar, and fish sauce. Pour over cabbage mixture. Toss to coat evenly, and chill until serving time.

MAKES 8 CUPS

CRANBERRY PECAN RELISH

You may experience difficulty going back to canned cranberry sauce after tasting this scrumptious Thanksgiving side dish.

¾ cup water
juice of ½ orange
⅓ cup sugar
⅓ cup honey
1 pound fresh *or* frozen cranberries
½ cup raisins
½ cup pecans, chopped

Combine the water, juice, sugar, and honey in a medium saucepan. Bring to a boil, reduce to a simmer, and add cranberries. Cook until the skins pop, about 5 minutes. Stir in raisins and pecans, and cook over medium heat until thickened to taste. Serve at room temperature or chilled.

SERVES 4 TO 8

YOGURT WITH HONEY
AND WALNUTS

*A simple favorite from the Greek restaurant
Sofi, in Los Angeles. Use good quality thick
plain yogurt and a richly flavored honey for
the full effect.*

¾ cup walnut halves and pieces, toasted
3 cups plain yogurt
1 to 2 tablespoons dark, thick honey
juice of ½ lime

Spread walnuts over shallow medium
ceramic or glass serving dish. Spread
yogurt evenly over top. Drizzle with
honey in zigzag pattern, and sprinkle with
lime. Cover, and chill until serving time.

SERVES 6

CLASSIC PESTO

Old-fashioned Italian-style basil and pine nut pesto is a standard in my summer kitchen.

2 cups basil leaves
2 garlic cloves, peeled
3 tablespoons pine nuts
½ cup olive oil
½ teaspoon coarse salt
½ cup grated Parmesan cheese

Combine basil, garlic, pine nuts, olive oil, and salt in a food processor. Purée until smooth, and transfer to a bowl. Beat in cheese with a spoon until a smooth paste forms.

Serve over hot pasta, with 1 or 2 spoonfuls of hot pasta water to thin the paste, or 1 tablespoon of butter for richness.

MAKES 1 CUP, ENOUGH FOR 1 POUND OF PASTA

SNOW PEAS WITH ALMONDS

*The thin shape of peas and almonds and their
simple goodness make this easy vegetable dish
an elegant choice for a dinner party.*

2 tablespoons butter
2 garlic cloves, thinly sliced
12 ounces snow peas, trimmed
⅓ cup sliced almonds
1 tablespoon soy sauce
salt and freshly ground pepper

Melt the butter in a large skillet over
medium-low heat. Cook the garlic to soft-
en, about 2 minutes. Add snow peas and
nuts. Turn the heat to high, and stir-fry to
coat peas evenly, about 2 minutes. Pour in
soy sauce, reduce heat, and cook less than
1 minute. Season to taste with salt and
pepper, and serve hot.

SERVES 4 TO 6

CASHEW BUTTER

For a change from traditional peanut butter and jelly—try this on sandwiches with apricot jam.

1 cup raw cashews, toasted
1 tablespoon peanut oil
2 teaspoons sugar
1 teaspoon salt

Combine all the ingredients in the food processor. Process until a paste, smooth or chunky, is formed. Store in the refrigerator as long as 2 months. Stir before serving.

MAKES 1 CUP

NUTS
FOR
DINNER

WALNUT SAUCE FOR PASTA

A luxurious sauce like this from Italy should be eaten with abandon—when calories play second fiddle to taste. Reduce by half for 1 pound of pasta.

2 garlic cloves
2 cups walnuts
½ cup pine nuts
2 cups half-and-half
2 tablespoons butter
2 tablespoons olive oil
coarse salt and freshly ground pepper

In a food processor, mince the garlic. Add the nuts, and purée until very fine. With the machine running, gradually pour in 1 cup half-and-half, 1 tablespoon of the butter, and all the oil. Process to combine.

Combine the remaining butter and half-and-half in a large skillet. Cook over high heat until reduced by half. Reduce heat to low, and whisk in the puréed nut mixture in batches. Whisk in salt and pepper to taste.

Serve hot with pasta, preferably a green spinach or herb noodle, or a cheese-stuffed pasta such as tortellini or ravioli.

MAKES ENOUGH FOR 2 POUNDS OF PASTA

KUNG PAU CHICKEN

*The traditional Chinese restaurant favorite
can be made with peanuts or cashews.*

¾ pound skinless, boneless chicken
    breast
1 tablespoon dry sherry
2 teaspoons soy sauce
1 tablespoon cornstarch
½ cup + 1 tablespoon peanut oil
1 cup raw cashews
1 tablespoon minced fresh ginger
1 tablespoon minced garlic
4 to 8 dried small red chiles, roughly
    chopped with seeds
1 bell pepper, seeded and cut into ½-inch
    cubes
3 scallions, cut in ½-inch slices

SAUCE
2 tablespoons soy sauce
2 tablespoons dry sherry
1 teaspoon sesame oil
½ teaspoon Chinese chile sauce

Cut chicken into ½-inch cubes. Place in bowl with sherry, soy sauce, and cornstarch. Toss to coat evenly, and refrigerate.

Heat ½ cup of oil in wok or large skillet over high heat. Fry cashews until golden, remove, and drain on paper towels. Carefully drain all but 2 tablespoons of oil from pan, and return to heat.

Stir-fry chicken just until white. Transfer with slotted spoon to platter.

Swirl remaining tablespoon of oil into pan. Briefly stir-fry ginger, garlic, and red chiles. Add bell pepper and scallions, and fry about 20 seconds longer. Pour in the sauce ingredients, chicken, and cashews. Stir and toss to combine, and tip out onto platter to serve.

SERVES 4

PECAN-CRUSTED CHICKEN

Sometimes we all need to feed the inner (or outer) child something really crunchy for dinner. With this cornflakes-and-nuts–encrusted chicken you can have the crunch without the fat of deep-frying. Lemon wedges or barbecue sauce for dipping are a nice complement.

2 cups crushed cornflakes
1 cup pecans, roughly chopped
¾ cup all-purpose flour
¼ teaspoon cumin
½ teaspoon paprika
pinch of cayenne
salt and freshly ground pepper
2 eggs
4 skinless, boneless chicken breast halves

Preheat oven to 400 degrees F.

Combine the cornflakes and pecans in a shallow bowl. Toss together the flour, cumin, paprika, cayenne, salt, and pepper in another shallow bowl. Beat the eggs in a third bowl.

Dip each chicken breast first in flour, patting off excess. Then dip in egg, shaking off excess, and transfer to pecan mixture. Pat to coat evenly, and transfer to baking dish. Bake about ½ hour. Serve hot.

SERVES 4

Pecans

Pecans are the second most popular nut in America, after the peanut. The fruit of a hickory tree, they are grown in the Southern states—home of classic American treats such as pralines and pecan pie. The word comes from the Native American paccan, *and* pakan, *for "nut."*

Pecans are always available in halves and pieces in the supermarket. They may be substituted for walnuts, though pecans have a bit more crunch and a distinctive flavor.

COLD PEANUT NOODLES

This is a great dish to have in your repertoire for hot weather cooking.

1 pound spaghettini, cooked, drained, and rinsed with cold water
4 tablespoons sesame oil
4 garlic cloves, peeled
2 (¼-inch) slices fresh ginger, peeled and crushed
¼ cup soy sauce
½ cup smooth peanut butter
¼ cup rice vinegar
¼ cup chicken stock
1 tablespoon Chinese chile oil
2 tablespoons brown sugar

Transfer pasta to large bowl, and toss with 2 tablespoons sesame oil to coat evenly.

Mince garlic and ginger in food processor or blender. Add 2 tablespoons sesame oil and remaining ingredients. Purée until smooth. Pour over noodles, toss well, and chill.

SERVES 4

CHICKEN PEANUT MOLE

Peanuts are a traditional feature of the nut-and-seed–based moles, or stews, from southern Mexico.

6 pounds chicken parts
6 dried chiles, such as California and ancho, wiped clean
2 large tomatoes
1 onion, unpeeled and halved
4 garlic cloves, unpeeled
½ cup raw peanuts
½ cup sesame seeds
¼ teaspoon fennel seeds
5 tablespoons vegetable oil
3 (1-inch) slices French *or* Italian white bread
1 cinnamon stick
salt and freshly ground pepper

Place chicken in stockpot with enough water to cover. Bring to a boil, reduce to a simmer, and cook, uncovered, 45 minutes.

Strain the broth and reserve the chicken. Set both aside.

Toast the chiles in a dry skillet over medium-low heat about 5 minutes. Remove, and discard the stems and seeds. Place the chiles in a large bowl. Pour in boiling water to cover, and let soak about 20 minutes.

Heat the broiler. Line a tray with foil, and place on it tomatoes, onion, and garlic. Broil, turning occasionally, until evenly charred. Peel the tomatoes, onion, and garlic.

In a food processor, combine the softened chiles, tomatoes, onion, and garlic. Purée until a paste is formed, and transfer to a bowl.

In the chile skillet, toast over low heat, one at a time: peanuts, sesame seeds, and fennel. Transfer to the food processor bowl.

Heat 3 tablespoons of the oil in the skillet. Fry the bread on both sides. Break into pieces, and place in food processor. Add

1 cup reserved chicken stock, and purée. Add chile mixture. Process until smooth.

Heat the remaining oil in a large Dutch oven over medium heat. Pour in the chile mixture, about 3 cups of reserved stock, cinnamon, salt, and pepper. Bring to a boil, reduce to a simmer, and cook until thickened to taste. Add chicken pieces, and simmer an additional 10 minutes to heat through. Ladle into bowls to serve.

SERVES 8

Peanuts

A peanut is a legume like the pea—a green plant that flowers aboveground and grows its fruits belowground in papery pods. The most popular snacking nut in the United States, the peanut originated in South America—in the areas now known as Brazil and Peru—and in the U.S. was first cultivated in South Carolina primarily as a food for the poor and for livestock. It was popularized in the early 20th century by Dr. George Washington Carver, who was a firm believer in peanuts—both as a cash crop and as a method for controlling the boll weevil.

African-Americans brought over as slaves were familiar with peanuts from Africa where they were introduced by the Portuguese and grew abundantly. Slaves referred to peanuts as "grober"—a twist on the Congolese word nguba. They also are known as "goobers," "ground nuts," and "monkey nuts."

The United States is the third-largest producer of peanuts in the world, after India and China. Because of their high quality, American peanuts are primarily used for eating. Four types of peanuts are grown in the South: runners, used for peanut butter; Virginias, with the largest kernels, for snacking; Spanish, little kernels covered with reddish brown skins and also used for snacking; and Valencias, which produce three or four small kernels to a pod and are used for making oil. Peanut oil has the highest burning point of any cooking oil.

For cooking, look for plain, unsalted peanuts, dry-roasted for extra crunch. When possible, purchase organic peanuts in the shell for snacking, since peanut crops are heavily sprayed.

SHRIMP PICADA

A paste of ground almonds with garlic and oil is a typical method from Spain for thickening and enriching a stew. Remaining picada may be kept in the refrigerator up to 1 week.

2½ ounces slivered almonds
3 garlic cloves
5 tablespoons olive oil
½ teaspoon saffron threads
½ teaspoon coarse salt
1 onion, chopped
2 tomatoes, seeded and chopped
½ cup chopped fresh Italian parsley
¼ teaspoon red chile flakes
2½ cups fish broth *or* clam juice
1½ pounds extra-large shrimp,
    in the shell

To make picada, combine the almonds, garlic, 3 tablespoons of the oil, saffron, and salt in a food processor. Purée to form a paste. Reserve.

Heat the remaining oil in a large, heavy pot over moderate heat. Cook the onion, tomatoes, parsley, and chile flakes until soft, about 7 minutes. Pour in the broth and bring to a boil. Stir in the shrimp and half the almond picada mixture. Reduce to a simmer, and cook until the shrimp are pink and curled, about 10 minutes. Ladle into bowls and serve hot with crusty bread for dipping.

SERVES 4

STUFFED VEAL WITH HAZELNUT BUTTER

Serve these rich rolls with a light green salad such as spinach or watercress.

8 slices veal scaloppini (about 1 pound)
salt and freshly ground pepper
¾ cup grated fontina *or* smoked
    mozzarella cheese
½ cup all-purpose flour
2 eggs, beaten
½ cup ground hazelnuts mixed with
    ¼ cup dry bread crumbs
3 tablespoons butter
lemon wedges for garnish

Lightly pound the veal to flatten. Season inside with salt and pepper, and sprinkle each with cheese in the center. Roll each veal slice along the width, enclosing the cheese and forming a tight cylinder. Secure with a toothpick.

Dip each veal roll first in the flour. Pat off excess, and then dip in the eggs. Roll in nut mixture to coat evenly. Place on plate, and chill at least ½ hour to set.

Preheat oven to 350 degrees F.

Melt the butter in a skillet over medium-low heat. Sauté the veal rolls until evenly browned. Transfer to a baking dish and bake 10 to 12 minutes, until veal is done and cheese is oozing. Serve hot with lemon wedges.

SERVES 4

Hazelnuts

Hazelnuts, also known as filberts, are small, round, dark brown nuts. An exceptionally crunchy and flavorful nut, the hazelnut is a popular choice for upscale pastries and confections in Western Europe and America. Its oil is considered a delicacy. Frangelico is a hazelnut-flavored liqueur.

The U.S. crop is primarily grown in Oregon and Washington state. In Europe it is found in the northern Mediterranean region.

Shelled filberts are sold in the supermarket baking section. Their dark brown skins can be removed by toasting in a 350-degree F oven about 20 minutes, until the skins crack and the nuts turn brown. Transfer hot nuts to a rough dish towel or strainer, a handful at a time, and rub to loosen skins. Do not be too finicky, as it is nearly impossible to do a perfect job.

NUT-RICH BREADS
AND
MUFFINS

TOASTED PECAN
SPICE WAFFLES

Nut lovers will find nothing to complain about with a breakfast of these pecan-packed beauties.

¾ cup all-purpose flour
1 teaspoon baking soda
1 teaspoon baking powder
½ teaspoon salt
2 tablespoons brown sugar
¼ teaspoon cinnamon
⅛ teaspoon ground ginger
1 cup buttermilk
2 eggs
1½ cups pecan halves, toasted
2 tablespoons butter, melted

Preheat the waffle iron.

Combine flour, baking soda and powder, salt, brown sugar, cinnamon, and ginger in large mixing bowl.

In another bowl, whisk together buttermilk and eggs. Pour into dry ingredients. Gently whisk to combine.

Finely chop ½ cup of the nuts and leave the rest whole. Stir chopped nuts and butter into the batter.

Pour onto the waffle iron and follow the manufacturer's instructions. Scatter remaining pecans over top, and serve with maple syrup.

SERVES 4

CURRANT WALNUT BAGUETTES

Serve this rustic fruit and nut bread with a selection of cheeses in the French style.

1 (¼-ounce) package yeast
1½ tablespoons honey
1¼ cups warm water
1½ cups bread flour
1½ cups whole wheat flour
1 teaspoon salt
¾ cup walnuts
¾ cup currants *or* golden raisins
butter for coating bowl
1 beaten egg for glaze

Stir together the yeast and honey in $\frac{1}{4}$ cup of the warm water. Let stand until foamy.

In a food processor fitted with a dough blade, combine the flours and salt. Process briefly. Add the walnuts, and process about 15 seconds more.

With the machine on, pour the yeast mixture through the feed tube. Slowly add the remaining water and continue processing until the dough clears the sides of the bowl and is no longer dry—about 1 minute.

Turn out onto a lightly floured board, and knead in the currants or raisins, about 5 minutes. Transfer to a bowl coated with butter and turn to coat evenly. Cover and let rise in a warm place until doubled, 1 to $1\frac{1}{2}$ hours.

Punch down dough on a lightly floured board, and divide into two parts. Roll each into a 6 x 15-inch sheet, and then into a long cylinder, pinching the edges to seal.

Transfer to a buttered baking sheet, cover, and set aside to rise until doubled again, about 45 minutes.

Preheat oven to 425 degrees F.

Brush the tops with beaten egg, and slash each with a sharp knife several times along the diagonal. Bake 30 to 40 minutes, until evenly browned and hollow when tapped.

MAKES 2 LOAVES

Walnuts

Walnuts—which can be traced back to 7000 B.C.—are one of the oldest tree foods known to civilization. This native of Southwestern Europe and Central Asia is grown today in California, Italy, France, and Germany. In France it is known as la noix—*"the nut"—because it is the nut most commonly used in cooking. Its oil is considered a delicacy.*

For cooking, shelled walnuts are available in pieces and halves year round in the baking section at the market. They are the most versatile nut for baking and are a standard pantry item for American favorites like chocolate chip cookies and brownies.

BANANA WALNUT PANCAKES

*Top these hearty flapjacks with warmed
maple syrup, additional chopped walnuts,
and sliced bananas for a true lumberjack
breakfast.*

1 ripe medium banana
1¼ cups low-fat milk
1 egg
1 teaspoon vanilla
1½ cups all-purpose flour
2 tablespoons sugar
1½ teaspoons baking powder
¼ teaspoon salt
¼ teaspoon cinnamon
½ cup walnuts, coarsely chopped
butter for coating

Place the banana, milk, egg, and vanilla in a blender. Pulse just to mash banana and blend.

In a large bowl, toss together flour, sugar, baking powder, salt, cinnamon, and walnuts. Add banana mixture to flour, and stir just until combined.

Heat the skillet or griddle over medium-high heat. Lightly coat with butter. Drop batter, ¼ cup at a time, on griddle, with plenty of space for spreading. Fry until bubbles form and break on the pancake's surface and the bottom is browned. Flip and cook just until done, about 1 minute longer.

MAKES 12

ONION WALNUT MUFFINS

The idea for these unusual savory muffins comes from the Thanksgiving dinner served by New York restaurateur Waldy Malouf.

1½ cups walnuts
2 medium onions, peeled and quartered
1 stick butter, melted and cooled
⅓ cup sugar
2 eggs
1½ teaspoons coarse salt
1½ teaspoons baking powder
1½ cups all-purpose flour

Preheat oven to 425 degrees F. Coat a muffin tin with cooking spray or line with paper cups.

Coarsely chop the walnuts in a food processor. Transfer to a small bowl. Add the onions to food processor, and purée until smooth. Transfer the onions to a large mixing bowl.

Stir the butter, sugar, and eggs into the onions. One at a time, stir in the salt, baking powder, walnuts, and flour. Stir until thoroughly combined. Spoon into muffin cups, and bake about 20 minutes, until a toothpick inserted in center comes out clean. Set aside to cool in the pan 10 minutes, and then turn out onto rack to cool. Muffins may be frozen and reheated at 350 degrees F. Serve warm.

MAKES 12

MACADAMIA CHIP CUPCAKES

Here is an upscale cupcake for the cappuccino crowd.

    1 stick butter, softened
    ¾ cup sugar
    2 eggs
    1 tablespoon vanilla
    1 cup half-and-half
    1½ cups all-purpose flour
    ½ cup + 2 tablespoons cake flour
    1 tablespoon baking powder
    ¼ teaspoon salt
    ½ cup macadamia nuts, toasted and
        chopped
    ¾ cup vanilla *or* white chocolate chips

Preheat oven to 350 degrees F. Grease muffin tins or line with paper cups.

Cream the butter until fluffy. Slowly add sugar, continuing to cream. Add eggs, one at a time, beating after each. Add vanilla and half-and-half. Beat until evenly blended.

In another bowl, mix together the two flours, baking powder, and salt. Add to liquid mixture, and beat just until flour disappears. Gently stir in nuts and chips. Fill muffin cups to the top, and bake 30 to 35 minutes until slightly golden on the edges and a tester comes out clean.

MAKES 12

Macadamia Nuts
Macadamia nuts are native to the rain forest in Queensland, Australia. Today Hawaii is the leading commercial grower.

In the market, this large, round, white nut is always found shelled. It is very rich, with a mild flavor and a great deal of crunch. Use a food processor or minichopper for chopping this tough nut.

Cashews

The cashew is the inside kernel of a kidney-shaped fruit found on a tropical evergreen grown in Africa, Asia, and South America. The shell of the fruit contains a poison, similar to that in poison ivy, that must be processed out before the kernel is removed. Due to that procedure and the kernel's kidney shape, removing cashews from the shell unbroken is a tricky and costly process.

SWEETS
AND
NUTS

PISTACHIO TORTE

This classic nut torte bakes to a beautiful golden-green hue from the natural pistachio coloring.

1½ sticks butter, softened
1 cup + 1 tablespoon sugar
5 eggs, separated
½ cup fine dry bread crumbs
1¾ cups raw pistachios, coarsely ground
confectioners' sugar for dusting
    (optional)

Preheat oven to 350 degrees F. Butter and flour a 9-inch springform pan.

Cream together butter and 1 cup of sugar until fluffy. Add the yolks, one at a time, beating well after each addition. Scrape down the bowl. Add the bread crumbs and the pistachios. Beat well to combine.

In another bowl, whisk the egg whites until soft peaks form. Add the remaining tablespoon of sugar, and continue whisking until stiff peaks form. Fold the whites into the pistachio mixture in three batches. Pour into the pan, smoothing the top with a spatula. Bake 45 to 50 minutes, until the center springs back when pressed and top is golden.

Cool in the pan on a rack 1 hour. Remove sides, and cool completely. Dust with confectioners' sugar if desired.

SERVES 8

Pistachios

Pistachios are world famous for snacking, since their shells are easy to pry open with the fingertips due to their natural "smile" or opening. A native of the Middle East, the pistachio is from the same botanical family as the cashew and the mango—the drupe group of plants. Their luxurious flavor and texture are key to baklava, nougat, and the renowned Italian ice cream.

PECAN PIE

*Thanksgiving dinner would not be complete
without this traditional favorite.*

1 recipe "Easy Tart Dough" (see page 94)

FILLING

2 eggs
1 egg yolk
¾ cup brown sugar
¾ cup dark corn syrup
3 tablespoons butter, melted
2 teaspoons vanilla extract
2 cups pecan halves, toasted

Roll out tart dough and line a 10-inch tart
pan with removable bottom. Pierce with a
fork, and chill at least ½ hour.

Preheat oven to 425 degrees F. Line the
tart shell with aluminum foil, fill with
weights or rice, and bake 10 minutes.
Remove, and reduce oven to 350 degrees F.

In a large bowl, whisk eggs and yolk until smooth. Add brown sugar, corn syrup, butter, and vanilla. Whisk until smooth.

Spread the pecans in the bottom of tart shell. Pour in filling, and bake until set, about 45 minutes.

SERVES 8

Pistachios

The California pistachio, which now rivals the Middle Eastern crop in size and quality, is brought to market green—its natural color rather than the traditional red color. Red dye is used to mask the red mottling that occurs in processing.

For cooking and baking, look for natural, unsalted, shelled pistachios. In California they can be found at Trader Joe's.

ALMOND MINICAKES

The pure flavor of almonds is a favorite of pastry makers around the world. This is a typical French confection.

1 cup whole blanched almonds, toasted
1½ cups confectioners' sugar
½ cup cake flour
pinch of salt
¾ cup egg whites
1½ sticks unsalted butter, melted

Preheat the oven to 450 degrees F. Generously butter a minimuffin pan.

Finely grind the almonds in a food processor. Add 1¼ cups sugar, flour, and salt. Process until well blended, and transfer to a mixing bowl.

Stir in the unbeaten egg whites and then the butter. Ladle the batter into the cups until two-thirds full. Bake 7 minutes. Reduce heat to 400 degrees F and bake 10 minutes longer. Turn the oven off and let sit in oven 5 minutes longer. (The muffins will be golden around the edges and peaked in the center.) Transfer pan to rack to cool 10 minutes. Invert to remove. When completely cool, sprinkle tops with remaining confectioners' sugar.

MAKES ABOUT 20

MAPLE WALNUT TART

The inspiration for this fantastic nut tart came from a class I took with master baker Jim Dodge.

1 recipe "Easy Tart Dough" (see page 94)

FILLING
1 cup maple syrup
1 cup brown sugar
3 tablespoons butter
1 tablespoon rum
1 teaspoon orange oil *or* 1 tablespoon grated orange zest
3 eggs
2½ cups walnut halves *or* pieces

Roll out tart dough and line a 10-inch tart pan with removable bottom. Pierce with a fork, and chill at least ½ hour.

Preheat oven to 425 degrees F. Line the tart shell with aluminum foil, fill with weights or rice, and bake 10 minutes. Remove, and reduce oven to 350 degrees F.

Combine the maple syrup, brown sugar, and butter in a heavy saucepan. Cook, stirring frequently, over low heat until butter melts and mixture is smooth. Remove from heat, stir in rum and orange oil or zest, and cool slightly.

In a large bowl, whisk eggs until smooth. Pour in maple syrup mixture and whisk until smooth.

Spread walnuts over tart shell. Pour on filling, and bake 45 to 55 minutes, until set.

SERVES 8

PECAN SHORTBREADS

A classic shortbread with a pecan pressed in the center for good measure!

2 sticks butter, softened
⅓ cup confectioners' sugar
⅓ cup brown sugar
2 teaspoons rum *or* vanilla extract
1 cup all-purpose flour
1¼ cups cake flour
½ teaspoon salt
¼ teaspoon cinnamon
24 pecan halves

Preheat oven to 350 degrees F.

In bowl of electric mixer, cream butter until light and fluffy. Add sugars and slowly beat to blend.

In another bowl, combine flours, salt, and cinnamon. Add to butter mixture, and mix until combined. Turn out onto floured board, press into circle, and lightly roll to ½-inch-thick circle.

Cut out with round cutters or small glass dipped in flour. Transfer cookies to ungreased cookie sheets, and press a pecan half in the center of each. Bake 18 to 20 minutes, just to set, not brown. Transfer to racks to cool. Re-roll remaining dough scraps, handling as briefly as possible, and cut out and bake remaining dough.

MAKES 24

HAZELNUT LINZER BARS

Here is an impressive, red jewel of a cookie to fill out a selection for tea.

1 stick butter, softened
⅓ cup sugar
1 egg yolk
2 teaspoons grated orange zest
1¼ cups all-purpose flour
½ cup finely ground toasted and peeled
　　hazelnuts
½ teaspoon baking powder
½ teaspoon cinnamon
¼ teaspoon ground cloves
pinch of salt
1 (10-ounce) jar raspberry preserves

Preheat oven to 350 degrees F.

Cream together butter and sugar until smooth. Beat in egg yolk and zest.

In another bowl, mix together flour, hazelnuts, baking powder, cinnamon, cloves, and salt. Add to the creamed butter, and gently beat until crumbly dough is formed. Press dough into an 8-inch-square baking pan, building up edges. Spread jam evenly over top. Bake 40 minutes. Cool on rack in pan. Cut into squares, lift out with spatula, and wrap in foil to store.

MAKES 20

MACADAMIA CUSTARDS

Chefs Mary Sue Milliken and Susan Feniger came up with this innovative method for infusing custard with a rich nutty flavor.

4 ounces macadamia nuts, toasted
   (1 cup)
2 cups heavy cream
½ cup sugar
2 eggs
2 egg yolks
1½ tablespoons rum *or* Kahlua

Finely grind the nuts in a food processor.

Bring the cream to a boil in a medium saucepan over medium-high heat. Stir in the sugar until dissolved. Stir in the macadamia nuts, bring back to a boil, and remove from heat. Let cool.

Preheat the oven to 325 degrees F.

In a large bowl, beat together the eggs and yolks until smooth. Slowly add the cream, stirring constantly. Stir in the rum or Kahlua. Strain the mixture through a fine sieve into a large glass measuring cup. Pour the custard into five 4-ounce ramekins and arrange in a large roasting pan. Pour boiling water halfway up the sides of the cups. Bake about 30 minutes, until set in the center. Remove from pan, and cool to room temperature. Chill until serving time.

SERVES 4

HAZELNUT NIBBLES

These nut-filled miniatures are a perfect light dessert.

½ stick butter, softened
3 tablespoons sugar
½ teaspoon vanilla extract
½ cup hazelnuts, toasted, peeled, and
    finely ground
½ cup all-purpose flour
sugar for sprinkling

Preheat oven to 300 degrees F.

Cream the butter and sugar together with an electric mixer until smooth. Beat in vanilla. Beat in nuts and then flour until a paste forms.

Break off teaspoon-size pieces of dough and roll between palms into balls. Place on uncoated baking sheet, and flatten slightly with a finger dipped in water. Bake about 30 minutes, until cookies are set but not brown. Transfer to racks and sprinkle the tops with sugar while warm.

MAKES 16 MINIATURES

MACADAMIA COCONUT CHEWS

Though many children are suspicious of nuts in their cookies, I've seen them swoon over this update on the standard chocolate chip cookie.

1 stick butter, softened
½ cup shortening
¾ cup sugar
¾ cup brown sugar
2 eggs
1½ teaspoons vanilla extract
2½ cups all-purpose flour
1 teaspoon baking powder
½ teaspoon salt
½ cup macadamias, toasted and roughly chopped
1 cup sweetened shredded coconut

Preheat oven to 350 degrees F. Lightly grease cookie sheets.

Cream together butter and shortening until light and smooth. Add sugars, and cream until light. Beat in eggs, one at a time, and then beat in vanilla.

In another bowl, stir together flour, baking powder, and salt. Add to creamed mixture and gently beat until flour disappears. Stir in macadamias and coconut.

Drop by tablespoonfuls, about 2 inches apart, on prepared sheets. Bake about 18 minutes, until edges are golden. Let sit 1 minute on sheet, then transfer to racks to cool.

MAKES ABOUT 36 COOKIES

Coconuts

Coconuts, the fruit of the tropical coconut palm, are prized worldwide for the exotic flavor and texture of their meat and the sweetness of their milk. Coconut is available fresh year round, but for easy access I purchase shredded natural, unsweetened coconut at the health food store or sweetened grated coconut in the supermarket baking section. Leftovers can always be kept in the freezer.

ALMOND PILLOWS

*I love a delicate cookie such as this along
with a selection of richer pastries for an after-
noon tea.*

2 recipes "Easy Tart Dough" (see page 94)
5 ounces prepared pure almond paste
2 eggs
flour for dusting
sliced almonds for sprinkling
confectioners' sugar for dusting

Prepare the dough, cut in half, wrap in
plastic, and chill at least 1 hour. Preheat
oven to 350 degrees F and line cookie
sheets with parchment.

Combine almond paste and 1 egg in
food processor, and process until smooth.
Transfer to small bowl. Beat remaining egg
in another small bowl.

On a floured board, with a floured pin, roll out dough one piece at a time, to ¼-inch thickness. Cut out 3-inch circles with cutter or glass. Fill each in the center with a teaspoonful of almond paste. Fold in half to make a semicircle, enclosing the filling. Pinch edges to seal, brush off excess flour, and transfer each pillow to prepared sheets.

Brush tops with beaten egg. Sprinkle with sliced almonds, pressing gently. Bake 20 to 25 minutes, until tops are golden. Transfer to racks, dust with confectioners' sugar, and cool. Repeat with second sheet, gathering up scraps and re-rolling each batch one time.

MAKES ABOUT 32

CASHEW MANDELBROT

Mandelbrot, the Jewish answer to biscotti, is updated with chunks of delectable cashews. It keeps well.

¾ cup cashews
½ cup vegetable oil
½ cup sugar
2 eggs
1 teaspoon vanilla extract
½ teaspoon almond extract
2 cups all-purpose flour
2 teaspoons baking powder
½ teaspoon cinnamon
¼ teaspoon salt

Preheat the oven to 350 degrees F. Toast the cashews. Finely grind ¼ cup, and coarsely chop ½ cup. Lightly grease baking sheet.

In a large bowl, whisk together oil and sugar. Whisk in eggs, vanilla, and almond extract.

In another bowl, combine flour, ground nuts, baking powder, cinnamon, and salt. Add to oil mixture and stir until flour just disappears. Stir in chopped nuts.

Gently knead on well-floured board and divide into four pieces. Pat each into a small loaf, about 3 x 5 inches. Transfer to prepared baking sheet and bake about 40 minutes, until edges are brown and center set. Remove, leaving oven on, and cool on cutting board 10 minutes.

With chef's knife, cut loaves across width into ½-inch slices. Return cookies to sheet, cut-side up, and bake an additional 8 minutes per side. Cool, and store in tins.

MAKES ABOUT 40

ALMOND TRUFFLES

These decadent chocolate-covered almonds have a high ratio of chocolate to nut.

1 pound bittersweet chocolate, roughly chopped
1 cup heavy cream
2 tablespoons amaretto
32 whole roasted almonds with skins
cocoa powder *or* chopped almonds for dusting

Melt the chocolate in a large stainless skillet over low heat, stirring constantly. When two-thirds of the chocolate has melted, remove from heat and continue stirring until smooth and glossy. Pour in cream and amaretto, and whisk until smooth.

Line a baking sheet with parchment. Pick up ½ tablespoonful of chocolate and drop an almond in the center. With the other hand, pick up another ½ tablespoonful chocolate and cover the almond.

Drop onto lined sheet and repeat. Refrigerate until nearly set, about 10 minutes. Lightly roll in cocoa or chopped nuts and return to sheet. Chill to set. Store in airtight container in the refrigerator.

MAKES ABOUT 32 LARGE TRUFFLES

Almonds

Almonds are an ancient nut from the Eastern Mediterranean region and Asia. The fruit of a tree similar botanically to a peach or plum tree, the almond comes in two types—bitter and sweet. Outlawed in the United States, the bitter almond—containing toxic prussic acid—is distilled for almond extract and cosmetics.

California produces one third of the world's almond crop today, with the remainder coming from Australia, Africa, and the Canary Islands. The island of Sicily produces the domestic Italian crop and is renowned in Italy for its almond confectionery.

SUGAR AND SPICE PECANS

These addictive sweet, crunchy treats are among the easiest sweets to make at home.

1 egg white
2 cups pecan halves
½ cup sugar
1 teaspoon cinnamon
½ teaspoon ground cloves
½ teaspoon ground nutmeg
½ teaspoon salt

Preheat the oven to 300 degrees F. Lightly butter a baking sheet.

Whisk the egg white in a mixing bowl until foamy. Add pecans and stir until evenly coated. Add sugar, cinnamon, cloves, nutmeg, and salt. Stir and toss until the nuts are evenly coated.

Turn the nuts out onto prepared pan, spreading to form a single layer. Bake 30 to 40 minutes. Break up and stir nuts with wooden spoon. Transfer to parchment or foil-lined counter to dry and cool. Store in tins.

MAKES 3 CUPS

Nuts and Health

Nuts are a highly concentrated source of protein and fat. In countries where animal protein is scarce, nuts are essential for protein. The fat in nuts is mostly polyunsaturated and monounsaturated—the types considered beneficial for lowering serum cholesterol and preventing heart disease. Because of their high fiber content, nuts are quite filling.

ALMOND TOFFEE

A crunchy, tooth-sticking goodie for the peanut brittle crowd!

butter for coating
1 stick butter
⅓ cup sugar
⅓ cup brown sugar
1 tablespoon light corn syrup
1 cup sliced almonds

Generously coat a baking tray and sharp paring knife with butter.

In a heavy saucepan, combine the butter, sugars, and corn syrup. Cook over medium-high heat, stirring frequently, until smooth. Raise heat to high and stir in almonds. Cook, stirring constantly, until the aroma of caramel is released, about 5 minutes. Immediately spread on coated sheet and cut into wedges with coated knife. Let set at room temperature about 1 hour. Separate pieces and store in sealed container.

MAKES ABOUT 20 PIECES

Almonds

For the home cook and baker, almonds are probably the most versatile nut. They are available in the supermarket in many varieties: whole roasted and blanched, slivered, and sliced. And their delicate flavor is distilled into extracts, oil, and the liqueur amaretto. Pure almond paste and marzipan are also available in the baking section. For homemade frangipane, or almond tart filling, see p. 95. These days, I prefer unsalted whole roasted almonds for snacking and cooking. With their brown skins on, they offer a bit more flavor and fiber.

EASY TART DOUGH

1 cup all-purpose flour
2 tablespoons sugar
pinch of salt
1 stick cold butter, cut into 8 pieces
1 egg yolk
1½ tablespoons cold water
½ teaspoon vanilla

Combine the flour, sugar, and salt in a food processor fitted with the metal blade. Process briefly. Add pieces of butter and pulse until large chunks of butter are visible.

In a small bowl, with a fork beat together egg yolk, water, and vanilla. With the food processor running, pour egg mixture through the feed tube and process until a dough ball forms on the blade. Press into disk, cover with plastic, and chill ½ hour or longer.

ENOUGH FOR ONE 10-INCH TART SHELL

FRANGIPANE

This homemade almond paste makes a terrific filling for an open fruit tart or a sumptuous spread for a toasted croissant.

1 cup whole blanched almonds
1 tablespoon all-purpose flour
1 stick butter, softened
½ cup sugar
2 egg yolks
1 teaspoon almond extract
pinch of salt

Combine the almonds and flour in food processor. Finely grind and transfer to a bowl.

Process the butter in the food processor until smooth. Add remaining ingredients, and process until fluffy. Add the ground almonds and combine with about 10 short pulses. Chill until firm. Store in a sealed container in the refrigerator as long as 1 week.

MAKES 1 CUP

CONVERSIONS

LIQUID
    1 Tbsp = 15 ml
    ½ cup = 4 fl oz = 125 ml
    1 cup = 8 fl oz = 250 ml

DRY
    ¼ cup = 4 Tbsp = 2 oz = 60 g
    1 cup = ½ pound = 8 oz = 250 g

FLOUR
    ½ cup = 60 g
    1 cup = 4 oz = 125 g

TEMPERATURE
    400° F = 200° C = gas mark 6
    375° F = 190° C = gas mark 5
    350° F = 175° C = gas mark 4

MISCELLANEOUS
    2 Tbsp butter = 1 oz = 30 g
    1 inch = 2.5 cm
    all-purpose flour = plain flour
    baking soda = bicarbonate of soda
    brown sugar = demerara sugar
    confectioners' sugar = icing sugar
    heavy cream = double cream
    molasses = black treacle
    raisins = sultanas
    rolled oats = oat flakes
    semisweet chocolate = plain chocolate
    sugar = caster sugar